C-E-O & M-O-M

Same Time Same Place

Rochelle B. Balch

Same Place

ISBN 0-9660468-0-3

Library of Congress Catalog Card Number: 97-94478

Manufactured and printed in Arizona, USA

Publisher

RB Balch & Associates, Inc.
PO BOX 10007
Glendale, Arizona 85318-0007

Editing

Lori Bruggeman, Karen Hedden, Andy Karpel

Cover Design, Illustrations

Running Changes, Phoenix, AZ. (602) 285-1834

Thank you APS for your continued support of small business

Table of Contents

Introduction

I founded RB Balch in early 1993 after being downsized out of my job—as a single mother in a new home. In a relatively short time, we have received city, state and national recognition—and created a two million dollar + home based computer consulting business.

With a lot of hard work, we have been able to attract a great group of consultants who work right along with us to help promote and market RB Balch. Actually, in the consulting business, your staff *is* your business. Starting as a one-employee firm, we have grown to over thirty employees; this, in itself, offers certain challenges.

Asked often about the secrets to my success, I wrote this book in an effort to help & encourage others in a similar situation. Being home based does not need to be the stepping stone to a "real office" outside of the house; for me, being home based *is* my "real office".

If you like, use this book as a workbook and take notes! Brainstorm! When you get an idea, write it down. If you think of something to do, write it down. If you think of something to check out, write it down. If you get bored (nah). Start thinking outside of the lines. Do something you normally don't do—write in the book! Section 10 to be exact. And, most of all, have fun.

Rochelle Balch

Call Me: (602) 561-9366
Fax Me: (602) 561-0012
See Me: www.rbbalch.com
E Me tm: rb@rbbalch.com

Acknowledgments

Thank you. Without your support and confidence my business would not be the success it is.

Glendale Public Library, Diane
Lucent Technologies, Susan, Mike, Max
Spartan Promotional Group, Alene
Streich Lang, Charles
The Arizona Business Gazette, Mike
The Arizona Republic, Jane
The Jewish News, Lee
Today's Arizona Women Success Magazine
Cindy, Charlotte, Eleanore
US West, Home Office Consultant, Dick
Wells Fargo, too many to mention

All of my friends I've met through **NAWBO (National Association of Women Business Owners). MJ, Patsy, Debbi, Patricia, Rosie, April, Debi, Mary Lou, Roma, RoseAnn, Adriana, Jill, Irene, Beti, Donna, Dave (yes, Dave)** and those I'm sure I forgot to mention. My good friends **Dave** and **Chris**, **Bea**, **Robin** and **Jeff**, and **Polly**.

The Arizona Department of Commerce-Arizona Business Connection & MWBE group, The Business Journal, Alpha Graphics, The Arrowhead Independent, Ranch Publications, Chambers of Commerce (Arizona, Phoenix, Glendale), Corporate Express, and the Glendale Parks & Recreation Department

A special thank you to Cecilia, Lorri and Bob of APS for your help.

And, a big thank you to my family and friends. My brother Andy started with me shortly after I started RB Balch, along with my mom, dad, Uncle Seymour, cousin Lori and a good friend, Karen. I could never have gotten to this point without their support and encouragement. My two girls, four cats and two dogs have also added to the experience.

A GIANT thank you to Shayna and Beth for understanding all of the times you've heard "get out of my office" from your dear ol' mom.

You want to get your business going, but . . . there are obstacles

It's only you

You don't have any customers

No one knows you

You're scared

What if you fail

These are only excuses because there is no passion—not yet.

Foreword

I had heard so much about Rochelle Balch that I felt like I knew her before I even met her. Her name and her business "appeared from nowhere" and both were suddenly featured at city, county and state committee meetings. Rochelle herself seemed to be everywhere at once, as a volunteer and as a sponsor. Soon RB Balch was in the newspapers and magazines and I found myself following her success, fascinated by this industrious woman who was building a business from scratch, supporting a family, and contributing to the community.

Previously, I had met Rochelle's mother and father, Edna and Harold, at a community event and had met her brother, Andy, at a Glendale Chamber of Commerce function. I learned that the entire family works for and is extremely supportive of RB Balch. By this time my curiosity was really strong.

I have finally met and talked with Rochelle. She is definitely a high-energy woman. One can't help but become enthusiastic and motivated by her. It is no wonder she has been able to accomplish so much in so little time. Rochelle has many experiences to share with all of us and C-E-O & M-O-M is a perfect way to do just that.

Elaine M. Scruggs
Mayor Glendale, Arizona

For Shayna and Beth
You can be what ever you want to be. Don't ever let someone tell you otherwise.

1 My Last Day is Friday

Getting It Together, Quick

You go to work every day. You do a good job. No, a very good job. You're dedicated. You work hard. You even miss a personal commitment or two to finish up some rush project. You think you are building a future for yourself and your family. Then, one day, in a flash, it's over. "Tough luck, but we had to cut back somewhere," they say. "Today is Wednesday. Friday is your last day." All I know is, I'm a single mom, in a new state and out of work.

I had moved to Phoenix from Irvine, California in early 1992. I bought a house, had a job with my employer from Irvine, and was making a good living. By Phoenix standards, actually, a very good living. Being single for many years, I was already preparing and saving for "the future". I had been out of a job once before in 1979 and decided then I would never again be without some money in the bank.

So, although I was instantly out of work, I had a little saved and knew I wouldn't starve. But, do you risk everything and go it alone—or get back into the regular work routine? This turned out to be quite a question for me. During this decision making time, intuitively, I started reducing my spending, watching for bargains and trying not to go to PriceCostco so often.

One day my daughter asked if she could still attend a school party (we're talking 3rd grade here) because it would cost "quite a bit—fifty cents". It hit me pretty hard then. I could take a pretty big risk, but I had to balance that with trying to retain some illusion of normalcy with my daughter. Of course, she went to the party, and good ol' Mom *took off work* to help out at school. I'm a single mom, in a new state, out of work, with a seven year old daughter.

Now, I've been in the computer business since 1968 and in the job placement and consulting business since 1979. I counsel people all the time about being out of work. I know I shouldn't blame myself, but, somehow, I found myself in that "I don't know what to do" mode for a little longer than I'd like.

Outwardly, I told everyone that I'm starting a business, but, really, for the first few months, I wasn't sure. The commitment wasn't there. The passion wasn't there—yet. I'm a single mom, in a new state, out of work, with a seven year old daughter, and no income.

So, what would I do if I was "at work" and had to start a new project? I would develop a plan. So that's what I did. But in this case, you call it a business plan. People said, "Write a business plan," so, naturally, I didn't want to do it. But, I found out real quick that I really needed to write it.

I know that I knew the business (that I wanted to be in) really well, since I had been doing it for years. The difference was, I was doing it for someone else before. I found that even though I knew what I wanted my business to be, when I put it down on paper, I really didn't have a plan on how to get there. And, I wasn't really sure I wanted to—really—deep down inside. I'm a single mom, in a new state, out of work, with a seven year old daughter, no income, trying to start a new business—am I crazy or what!

But, then it clicked. I did want to do this. I did not want to ever be dependent on "them" again. The passion had arrived. So, I started the plan—for real. To get from A to B (from out of work to being a successful business owner), is more like going from A to Z; there's a lot in between to get to where you want to go. Writing it down, forcing me to think, helped. For me, my business would be sub-contracting computer professionals to large corporations and basically making my money from each hour they worked. Great, but before I had all of these employees, I needed to generate income. So, I billed myself out to smaller companies to help set up computers, software programs, and whatever. This got me going.

Meanwhile, I was marketing and still working on my plan. Then, when I hired my first full-time employee, I was committed.

I think what has helped me the most in becoming successful is that I knew I would succeed from the beginning. I set up my business as if it were already an up-and-running successful business. I set up my computer systems and databases for tracking clients and appointments, etc., I set up office procedures (yes, just for myself), and I had confidence and enthusiasm dripping from my veins. You have to. If you're not confident, no one else is going to have confidence in you or buy from you.

What I'm trying to tell you here is that even when you think you are doing something, you still may not be *really* doing it. I *say* I started my business in February, 1993 (and I did), but I really wasn't *committed* until about June, 1993. I just wanted to mention this little fact in case you have the same feelings—you're not alone.

It's there, you made the pole. Just reach for it.

2 Pat Your Head & Rub Your Tummy

You can do it. Just hope a fly doesn't land on your nose.

Women can do it. We can do multiple things at one time. We can cook dinner, answer the phone and break up a fight between the kids at the same time. We can work on a proposal, confer with a colleague, fax a memo, and sign a letter at the same time. We can be working on the computer, sign for a package delivery or a school permission slip and be on the phone at the same time. Get the picture?

We've been trained to do more than one thing at a time. And that's the difference in being successful or not. What?

If we *can* do a lot of things at once, then *do we* do a lot of things at once? If we have the initiative, the passion, the commitment to succeed, then we can do it. Many of us just take the easy way out and say we're too busy, or we just can't add one more thing, or whatever. Through the cultural and traditional backgrounds we come from, we are trained to be mothers - whether we want to or not. In doing that, we learn to juggle things, do multiple tasks and, most importantly, prioritize.

I'm always telling my girls, "Don't be a dweller. Deal with it and move on." It's easy to let obstacles get in the way. Nothing is so big that we can't deal with it, although sometimes we may need a little help with defining and analyzing the options. We know we can juggle. We know we can prioritize. We know we can make decisions. So, when an *opportunity* presents itself—deal with it, and move on.

Did I have time to write this book? Not really. In the beginning, I started fooling around with the idea (10/26/96 to be exact). I worked on it a little and then used the "I don't have time" excuse. My brother was asking "How's the book coming?" Then I started thinking about some things I'd heard at a couple of meetings. "Why not do it? And why not now?" and "To grow your business, work on your business, not in your business as much." That gave me the extra push I needed, and *wa-la,* here it is—the book. Somehow, I was able to prioritize, juggle, move on, and get this done—because I wanted to.

I believe that balancing and prioritizing are two different things. When someone asks how do you balance your work and your personal life, I must admit, I don't. I don't think you can equally balance the role of mother, wife or significant other, business woman, volunteer, etc. There are just times when you need to spend time doing one of the above. What I do, though, is prioritize. You've heard the expression *get your priorities straight.* For me, my priorities are first my family (my daughters, then the rest), my business, then volunteer work for the community.

Prioritizing makes it easier for me not to be in balance all of the time. I know I can take a day and go on a field trip at school or take a short trip with the kids and not feel guilty about work. On the other hand, I may work all night or long hours to finish a project, and then *veg-out* and watch TV.

Part of prioritizing for me has also been to keep my business in my house. I could maybe grow faster and become bigger sooner in an outside office, but my first priority is me and my family. I like being home in the morning when the kids get ready for school, and, as much as I complain about taking Shayna and Beth to the bus stop, I like being here so I can take them. I like to be home when they get home from school. Even if I'm working and telling them to "get out," I'm still here in the house, and that's important for me. As a result, I don't do early morning or late afternoon meetings.

Maybe, someday, they'll want to run a business of their own, watching mom and all. What am I saying? Shayna already knows she wants to *be the boss*. She wants to have her own office or store, with a back room, where she goes, and no one else can; Shayna wants to be a either a veterinarian with a pet shop, or a pediatrician. Beth, at first wanting to become a masseuse, is now looking at becoming a biologist and setting up habitats for living and experimenting. I guess some of it rubs off.

So, can you run a business and have a personal life? I think so. Do you?

How many things can you do at once? Now add 3.

3 It's OK to Toot Your Own Horn And You Should

I, personally, did not want to wait three to five years to look big. I wanted potential clients to ***assume*** that RB Balch was already big and established, unless ***I*** told them otherwise. And the approach seems to be working.

If you think it, you become it. I truly believe that if you act successful, you become successful. First, let's define success. What is success? What is successful for me may be different for you. Is success money? Is success property? Is success a spouse? Is success having children? What is it for you?

For me, success is financial and personal security for myself and my family. That is, I want to make enough money to make my house payments, to have a little fun, to have some money in the bank earning interest and growing for retirement, and feel that I am responsible for my own destiny.

Am I successful? I think so. I started saving money years ago. $10 here, $20 there, sometimes $100 at once. Little by little it adds up. If I had waited to start saving until I thought I could afford it, I never would have begun. You just do it. Just like a new business owner—just do it.

A friend of mine, a single mom, has a great job. She makes lots (and I mean lots) of money. She loves what she does at work. But, she is unhappy. She does not feel successful. Why? Because she finally figured out that success for her was being able to spend more time at home with her young daughter. With her current job—as much as she likes it—she can't do that; she works well over 60 hours a week and does some overnight traveling. So what should she do? Get her priorities straight! She knows them, now she is putting them in order. She will either change her work pattern (leave after eight hours a couple of times a week and come in a little later in the morning) or change her job—even if it means less pay. This woman figured out that success for her was not money, but success was being able to spend more time as a parent. BTW (that's Internet lingo for "by the way"), I think she is going to move to be closer to her family and find a job that fits her goals, objectives, and priorities.

If I know that I'm successful, do others know it too? Should I tell them? You're darn right I should. My mom told me a long time ago, "If you don't speak up, no one knows what you're thinking." Now, I admit, I might take that advice a little far sometimes, because, generally people know how I feel about certain issues and situations.

I started a mailing campaign very early on, as I'm a believer in *if you see it enough, you think it must be good.* I have been mailing *something* to my clients, and potential clients, since the beginning, about every 6 to 8 weeks. When people see things enough, they respond with "I've seen that" or "I've heard of them." So why not let that "them" be YOU. If I mail something, and even if the recipient doesn't open the letter, my name and logo went across their desk. That's worth the postage right there for me. If they open it up, even better. If what you mail is interesting, people begin to anticipate something in the mail and actually look forward to receiving the next mailing. Try to make direct mail items different—not all sales literature.

Some of the items we've mailed include:

Tip Cards (Quick helpful hints about PCs, Windows, E-Mail, and so on)

Information Newsletters about a particular topic

Copy of our Employee Newsletter

Reprints of news articles where we're mentioned

A large paper clip, with logo, of course

New Address cards (when we moved)

Event sponsorship, community activities flyers

Volunteer activities available

Write a press release and send it to everyone. If you're *going to have* a success, talk about it. If *you have* a success, talk about it AND write about it. And send it to everyone. That includes both neighborhood and city newspapers, organizations you belong to or volunteer for, the Chamber of Commerce, and more. You'll be surprised who reads what.

Write an article about something relevant to your industry and mail it out to your mailing list or to some of the smaller newspapers. It's pretty cool when you see it in print. It really isn't that hard—

it just takes a little time and effort. The rewards are terrific.

Once something is published, get permission and reprint it and then send it out to everyone. Include clients, potential clients, and all of your vendors, such as your accountant, banker, attorney, printer, etc.

Let people know what you are doing. Don't be afraid to show enthusiasm about a new business deal. You'll find that enthusiasm is contagious and people like to be around enthusiastic and motivating people.

I remember very clearly nominating myself and my company for six major awards in a 12-month period. The reactions I got went from sheer disbelief that I would actually nominate myself (what nerve), to "you really should never nominate yourself because judges don't like it." From the six contests, we won first place for two, were named as finalists for two, and got thank-you letters from two. Now, I think that's pretty darn good. You know yourself and your business better than anyone, so why not toot your own horn.

By the way, of the two contests we got thank yous from, we entered them again the next year. For one (of the two), we were named as a finalist, and then won! And we're still ready to keep on entering. It takes a little time, but you also get your name in the paper. So, why not?

Get your name out there. I have my logo on *everything* and we distribute things *everywhere.* Pencils, pencil cups, pens, note pads, mouse pads, tape dispensers, t-shirts and more. I want people to see the image, know the company, ***perceive our success while we achieve it*** and, most of all, call us for business.

Let me tell you about our t-shirts. We (my brother and I) were going to a large computer show in Las Vegas and kidded about wearing a sign telling everyone what we did. Well, that turned into one of our biggest hits ever. We created our much sought after black and white t-shirt. On the back, they proclaim 'Contract Programming', along with our slogan 'Call Me, Fax Me, See Me, E-Me'tm and our home page (web site) address (www. rbbalch.com), 800 number (1-800-9-BALCH-9) and local phone number. The t-shirts and slogans got so popular that we trademarked both the slogan and logo.

Everyone thought we were a huge company and were in disbelief that we would actually advertise ourselves so boldly like that. Now, we get "sighting calls" from all over. When someone spots our t-shirt (or other logo item), they call us. We've collected some good stories. One of my favorites happened to someone signing in at a campground in the mountains. The man behind the desk gave them an RB Balch pen to sign-in! How did it get there?. And what about wearing our t-shirts to the grocery store, mall or park? Toot, toot.

When I started with my give aways, I wanted something I could hand out freely; something not too expensive, but something that looked good and added to the "we're successful image." I started with pens (under $1 each) and then note pads (about$.50 each). I added pencils (500 for $100). I found someone who would let me order in small quantities (100 to 300 items at a time). Now, I order larger amounts, but in the beginning, I couldn't afford to do that. This particular vendor, by the way, was one of my first clients; I helped her set up computers in her office, thinking "someday I'll be big enough to order promotional items myself and be her customer." Pretty quickly after we started with our promotional items, our response went from "who" to "oh, you guys."

Another way to get out there and toot your horn is to *piggy back* on another activity. If I sponsor an event, or volunteer as a speaker or panelist, my name is mentioned in their promotional activities. Someone at a meeting one time thought that the *piggy-back* method was like being a *leach*. I don't think so; I think it's a smart way to stretch your advertising and promotional dollars and to build up your visibility.

Act successful to be successful, and then don't forget to tell someone about it.

Don't forget to tell someone about your success.

4 Create the Image

Looking Bigger than you are

Create it. Package it. Promote it. Sell it.

What kind of business do you want? Formal, casual, funny, stuffy. What? Create the image.

For me, I want a professional, casual, easy-to-reach image and atmosphere.

What is included to create the image? Everything. From your business cards, letterhead, type of pen you use, clothes you wear, car you drive, and restaurants you visit.

You've heard it before, "you've only got one chance to make a first impression?" It's true, and always remember it.

Let's start with the professional part. We'll assume, as entrepreneurs, we want a professional image. Do you have a good computer and laser printer? A good phone system, with some type of reliable phone messaging? A good copier? Note pads or some type of informal stationery for a quick note? These are all little things that add to the image and how you are perceived.

For about the first one and one-half years, I was using white, glossy presentation folders that I got at a stationery store, printed labels with my logo, and put them neatly in the lower right hand corner. I used the folders for proposals and presenting information about my company to potential and existing clients. I thought they looked just fine. And they did, until one day when I asked for some feedback from a client. He thought everything inside looked great and the idea was fine. Problem. The label on the folder he had received was slightly crooked. It ruined the whole image. Although it was expensive (and not something I thought I could afford at the time), I decided I couldn't afford *not* to print up professional folders.

I had to print up 1,000 folders to get a decent price. My next problem was that I moved two years later and still had plenty of folders left over—and I had put my address along the bottom on the back. To use the supply of these folders, we're now putting labels, printed with a *text cloud* with the words "New address, Same great service" and our PO Box over the old address. For our image, the folder is professional, the label says "we're casual and cost conscious." And we're very careful to line it up straight along the bottom.

Do you advertise? Where? I personally like the direct, but indirect approach. I like to catch people with my logo when they're not necessarily expecting it. Try ads in local papers, group directories, and at community activity events, not just in the local business journal type newspapers or magazines. Even if you run classified ads to hire people, clients and potential clients are reading the ads too.

I like to advertise in unusual places. How about the local school district newspaper or an ad in a special pull-out section of the Sunday paper.

Some things look expensive and are, but many others are surprisingly affordable. The big local newspaper annually runs a special business section, highlighting businesses and discussing the general business climate. They put in a special section for biographies of businesses, by date founded. I first came across this promotional opportunity in 1994 and for $100, I was able to be listed, along with the big guys, in a nice ad. It looked like I had been specially selected to be included under 1993; I was, of course, selected—after I sent in my $100. And, of course, I continue to be "selected" every year.

I'm creating my image and, remember, I want mine to be professional, but fun and casual too. Be creative, look for deals. Don't be afraid to ask for discounts; I do all the time—and it works many times.

Get involved in community activities and volunteer. Not only will you feel very good about doing something for someone else, it's great visibility. I had one target account that would never call me back; then, one day, months later, he did. When I asked "why did you finally call me back," he said he had seen where we sponsored an event that he was interested in and thought the least he could do was to call me back.

And don't forget the publicity that comes with volunteering or being a sponsor. Many times you will get TV, radio, newsletters, newspapers and other advertising FREE as a result. Remember, the organization you've volunteered for is heavily promoting their event. If you're generous enough to volunteer or accept an invitation to be a speaker, seminar provider or panelist, you'll probably have your name and business included in some type of wide-spread mailing campaign.

But, don't get me wrong. You don't volunteer because you expect to get recognition in return. You volunteer because it's good and because you should. Volunteering is worthwhile. And, not to sound too corny, personally, it is very rewarding.

Sponsor a fun event—create you own image. I like country music. For 1997, we had an opportunity to sponsor a family rodeo (yes, a rodeo). This was a pretty big commitment, but I believe it will be a good investment in the future of my business, as well as donating money to a good cause. Plus, we're having lots of fun with the whole concept.

How do you dress? You can dress professionally and not be in a suit. I can't handle suits anymore. I prefer a nice comfortable (usually cotton) dress, or a denim skirt and shirt with cowboy boots. Of course, you should dress as appropriate for the environment and client too, but your personality and your company's personality will come through.

What about promotional items? I decided that I wanted my name always in front of my client. So I design my promotional items around desk items.

We started with a pencil cup and have created many items that go into it (pen, pencil, ruler, staple remover, letter opener, flashlight, etc.). In addition, we have folder holders, tape dispensers, paper-clips holders and more. I never want my client to forget our name or our phone number. All of the items are made from nice quality white and black plastic. Nice, but not gaudy. Nice, but not too expensive. Nice, and not too obnoxious. So far, so good. People just love our pens (the only non-black-and-white item—they're bright purple).

Our clients and staff are always asking "what's next—luggage, a boat, what?" As a joke one year, my brother took a large mail-order catalog and taped a new cover to the front - "RB Balch Gift Catalog." He had lots of fun just carrying it with him at different accounts.

We believe that we have created the image we want. A small, successful, fun, entrepreneurial company, with management that is easily reached.

Let me tell you all
about my success...
it all started when
1st

5 the House Rules

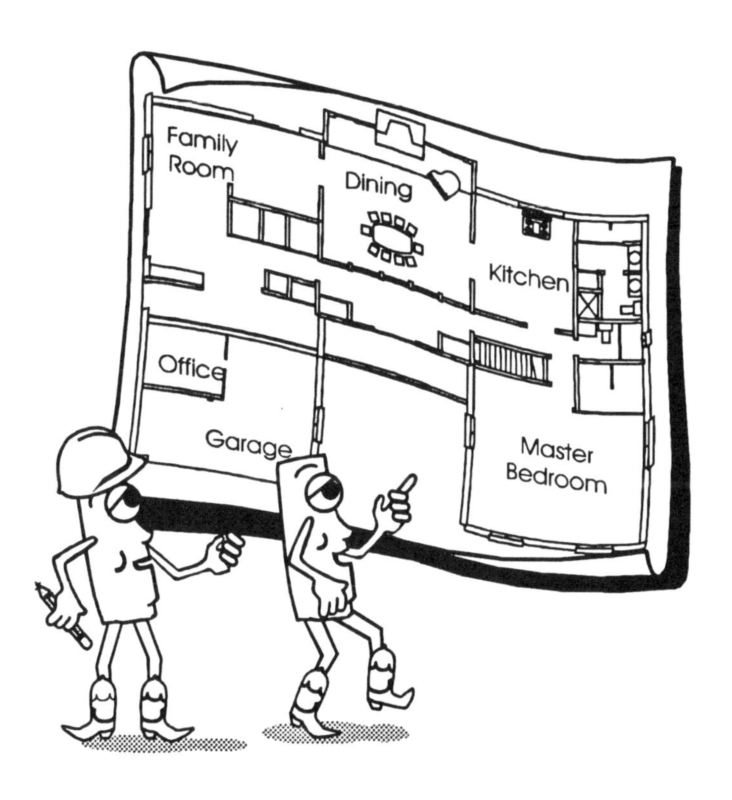

FYI, our 4th year sales were over $2 million. I thought it was time I added that piece of information. When people hear about businesses that are based out of a home, right away they think, "Isn't that cute." That's fine. But that's when I like to add the part about how big we have gotten. That quiets them right down.

People me ask, "When are you going to move into a real office?" Why do they do that? I like being **C-E-O & M-O-M**, at the same time and in the same place. And my plans are to stay that way. Depending on the business, home based does not automatically mean that the business is small and just getting started. You can be based at home and get as big as you want to.

It's the image and level of professionalism that is projected, and quality of the service or products that allows you to succeed.

Of course, you must believe this. Are you working at home for the day or is your business based out of your home? It's important to understand this difference and to present yourself and company accordingly.

I've had an office in my home since I've been a mother. Sometimes, if I got stuck with my babysitter, I would bring Shayna to work with me (fortunately, I was in an office where I could do that). As I got into consulting and sales, I found that I could work at home better than away in an office. There were no distractions and I liked being home with my daughter (I still had a babysitter). However, big business wasn't ready for the "home office" back in the 1980's, so I've been fighting the "home office" battle a long time. Today, the concept (how unique), is more and more accepted. Even if you normally work elsewhere (and are not a business owner), sometimes, just being able to have an office from your home to work at when you like is enough. It can really add to your "I am successful, I am happy" attitude.

To work based out of the house, there have to be certain house rules. There will, of course, be times when you want to give the *illusion* of a formal office and other times when it seems OK to be home based.

Some our the guidelines (notice I changed that to guidelines from rules, since, as we all know, rules are meant to be broken} in my house include:

1. This is a business. Everyone, and I mean, *everyone*, in the family needs to know and understand that you run a business from your home; you are not simply working at home for the day. In my house, even the neighborhood kids that come over understand about *no running or shouting down the halls.*

2. The Phones. No kids. Period. Never let anyone other than a 'phone trained' adult answer your business phone. There are no exceptions to this rule. Invest in voice mail or in an excellent quality answering machine or answering service. Your customers expect it. You already know the line about "you only have one chance to make a first impression."

3. Separate room. You must have a separate place to work. Setting up on the kitchen table everyday really won't work. Working in the family room, with the TV on, is not exactly a productive spot. If you don't have a separate room, try a nice spot in your bedroom. And, if you have dogs (that bark), a door is a must.

4. Noise control. No TV's, stereos, CD's, radios, or video movies louder than the room in which they are playing in. Musical instrument, cheerleading, or

band practice, must be in a room other than your office, with the door closed.

5. Equipment. Your equipment must be ready and in good condition at all times. During business hours, the business has priority for all equipment. Other family members need to schedule their time to use any equipment before or after work.

   A professional image is critical to success. Invest in a good quality printer, connected to your reliable, dependable, adequate (or better) computer. Don't forget office supplies, file cabinets, good lighting, a desk and good chair. Consider a postage meter when your postage grows (I got mine when I was spending over about $250 per month). If appropriate, consider a copier, and modem. And, if you use your computer a lot, strongly consider some type of backup unit and battery backup (in case the power goes out; this is different from a surge protector).

(I had to mention the computer stuff. After all, I'm in the computer business).

6. Act like a business. Get out of the house. Don't forget to go to networking events (to meet people and to be seen) and visit clients (if appropriate). And get out and volunteer. Be involved in the community.

And don't forget to check with the city in which you live; make sure you're within *their* guidelines. Be considerate and careful about who comes to your home. Many cities do not allow customers or clients to come to the house because neighbors do not want commercial traffic in their neighborhood. Some cities allow for family members only to be employees of home based businesses.

For me, this business is perfect, as our clients do not come to our office—I go to them. And, with my family, they'd be at my house whether or not I had something for them to do.

6 You're it. No one else to blame

C-E-O, you wanted it. You got it. Now do it.

Running your own business is definitely not the same as working for someone else.

You plan it, you do it, you're responsible for it. There is no one else but you. Sound scary? It is. Sound like hard work? It is. Sound like fun? It is.

Think about it. You're the client. You have a problem. You call your vendor. The receptionist passes you along to a customer service representative. That person passes you to the supervisor. Then on to the manager, maybe to the general manager. Have you ever talked to the owner? Probably not. These people all work there; although they get a pay check, their entire livelihood does not depend on their own response. They could simply '"pass the buck."

As a small business owner when there is a problem or situation to deal with, most likely, the client can talk directly with you. Your livelihood *does* depend on your response. There is no buck to pass.

This scenario can really be used to your advantage. Besides the fact that it's true, why not use it as a marketing tool. You care, it's your business, you wouldn't be in business if wasn't for great customers like them.

You've heard it before, but you really do need to build good business partnerships. Business to business. Decision maker to decision maker. Take the responsibility and run with it. And let your customer know it.

Many times, when I'm having a hard time reaching a client, I'll leave my home phone number in a voice mail or e-mail. They usually don't call me at home, but they know they could—and the next time they seem a little easier to reach.

Can you do it alone? No. You need to establish good relationships with others, like the banker, the printer, the accountant, the office supplier, the attorney, the baker (oops), the local florist. We occasionally use the florist or a home-baked cookie business for a nice "thank you" or "congratulations" for someone.

What about office help? Eventually, you may get to the point where you just need help in the office. Administrative help for office stuff, payroll, invoicing, etc.

This was a big decision for me. Do I continue to work all hours (at least two shifts) or hire someone and concentrate on selling. I knew I would not grow any more if I didn't add some help. After all, it was money out of my pocket—literally.

It only hurt for awhile. Then I realized how more productive I could be with someone helping me. In my case, this help now includes my brother, uncle, cousin, a close friend, and my mom and dad.

However, involving family in your business is a whole other story. In my family, we've discussed it many times—but you need too—if you hire a family member outside of your immediate live-in family. You work harder than anyone else and you expect to make more money. Others, especially family, see this and sometimes jealousies can arise. I strongly suggest that if you hire family, you discuss this up front. Everyone needs to have their own goals and objectives in place. By the way, one of my personal goals is to be on a national talk show (so watch for me some day).

What about employees that are not family members? How do you know if you've picked the right person? In our family when someone wants to put *dibs* on something, my dad will say "Is your name on it?" If the answer is "yes," then it's yours.

My daughter, Shayna, learned quickly to always answer "yes."

In my case, my name is *in* my business, *on* my business and *is* my business. So I want to be careful about who we print business cards for. For a relatively few dollars, we provide drug testing and background checking (criminal, education and employment) for all new employees. Not only do we feel better about our staff, I believe that our staff feels better knowing that this type of checking is performed for everyone.

And remember, company attitude begins at the top. For me, the "*CO*", I am the top. "*CO?*" Yes, "*CO*". Commanding Officer. My dad affectionately calls me the "*CO*". Actually, I guess, when you're the CEO *and* the mom, it makes you pretty much in command.

Running your own business and being independent can be great and lots of fun, but never forget—you're it—there's no else to blame.

PROBLEM
CHALLENGE
FUN
CO

7 FAQ's

FYI. Here are some questions people ask me most frequently. Maybe you wanted to ask too.

1. When did you get "downsized" out and start your business?

   Downsized out 01/28/93. Started my business, 02/01/93. Committed to my business 06/93.

2. How much did you invest initially? From where? And for what?

$5,000, part of a small severance package from my previous employer. I used it for stationery, business cards, flyers, a little brochure, presentation folders, and office supplies. Also I used it to upgrade some computer software packages (fortunately, I had just recently upgraded my computer system). Selectively, I had some client/potential client lunch meetings.

3. When did you start taking money out for a salary for yourself?

After about 8 months I started taking out a salary of $200 a week.

4. When did you start making "good" money?

The third year.

5. How do you balance home and business?

I don't. I prioritize. One side usually takes precedent over the other for a while—for a specific period of time. For example, I tell the kids, I'm working until 8 PM tonight, then, we'll watch a show together.

This morning, we did registration at school, then out to lunch (to celebrate going back to school—sort of); I'll work half a day today. I don't feel guilty about it, as I worked until 10:30 PM last night.

Sometimes it's hard, and, at times, I do have to work at keeping my priorities straight.

6. How do you find time for all of the volunteer work?

You just make the time. I like to volunteer for things that require short, contained amounts of time. I don't usually volunteer for activities that require long and lengthy time commitments. Except for Junior Achievement, which runs for 6 weeks, I do lots of "one shot" things.

And, oh yes, one other full-time commitment; I'm a foster mom too.

7. Why do you volunteer so much?

It's fun, it helps someone and it makes good sense. And, if I'm speaking, it's good practice to get up in front a group (5 to 500). You never know when an opportunity may arise—like maybe being named for an award or something—and public speaking experience is very helpful.

And, of course, it gets our name out there even more. Tonight I'm giving a free two hour seminar at the library; this week I've seen our

name listed in three newspapers, promoting the seminar.

8. Isn't the promotional stuff expensive?

It can be. You need to look around and find a vendor or distributor who will work with you and within your budget. Look for deals. Buy in small quantities to test your item, and be a little selective in giving it away at first. You'll quickly see that it IS a good investment.

9. Do you have a bank loan? Was it hard to get?

Yes. Yes.

I have a line of credit; I use it when I need it, then pay it down and use it again. I need it for payroll. I pay my staff before I get paid from my client. Our business is providing labor to our clients.

The bank said "No" at first. I was definitely *assertive.* I wouldn't take "No" for an answer. I was insistent that they sit with me to understand my business and review my business plan, not just make a decision based on an application and a set of bank rules. After they "happily" (not) agreed to meet with me, I got a small line of credit (that has since increased). I do admit, however, that it certainly helped that I had good personal credit and did have a small savings account and a retirement account. I looked like a "good risk."

When someone tells me No, it just means to me that I have to re-address the situation and ask the question another way.

10. Do you ever want to go give up the headaches and just go back to working for someone else again?

A definite NO. If I have a headache, I'll take an aspirin. I like being in control of my own destiny.

11. Can you really have a successful home based business *and* have time for your family *and* keep your sanity?

    Yes! Just learn how to juggle.

Tips for Keeping Your Sanity

1. Keep everything in perspective.

2. Don't let little things get in the way.

3. Don't try to fix everything. Let some things work themselves out.

4. Keep focused.

5. Don't let others intimidate you. Once you start to defend yourself, you lose.

6. Watch expenses and make changes when necessary.

7. Know the business you're in and keep reminding yourself what it is.

8. Define success for yourself, don't use someone else's definition.

9. Set an obtainable goal, write it down, review it, and work towards it.

10. Stay confident, keep honest and remain professional.

8 People to See, Things to Do

No time to waste.

Start to get ready, and then get ready to start. There are lots of people to see and things to do. Over the next few pages, I've included some lists I use and some actual pieces from my business plan. Maybe some of this will be helpful and get you started. After I wrote my outlines, I found it was easier to get going.

Important Names & Numbers

(you many need to verify phone numbers)

I use this list when I teach business startup classes. Most of these numbers are for the Phoenix, Arizona area; if you're in another area, use this as a checklist and reminder of things you need for your area. Just check in your local phone book for comparable listings.

Arizona Business Gazette	271-7300
Arizona Chamber of Commerce	248-9172
Arizona Corporation Commission	542-3026
Arizona Dept. of Commerce Arizona Business Connection	280-1480
Arizona Dept. of Economic Security (State Unemployment Tax)	255-4807
Arizona Dept. of Immigration	379-3804
Arizona Dept. of Labor	640-2990
Arizona Dept. of Revenue Sales Tax	542-4576

Arizona Dept. of Revenue Withholding Taxes	542-4576
Arizona Secretary of State Trade name, Trade mark	542-6187
Arizona Small Business Association	265-4563
City of Glendale	435-4169
City of Phoenix Small Business Assistance	262-5040
City of Phoenix, MWBE Office	262-6790
Glendale Chamber of Commerce	937-4754
Internal Revenue Service	1-800-TAX-FORM
Phoenix Chamber of Commerce	495-2195
SCORE (part of SBA)	640-2329
Self Employment Loan Fund	340-8953
Small Business Association (SBA)	640-2316
State Fund/Workers' Comp.	939-3366
The Arizona Republic (main) City desk (press release)	444-8000 444-8222

The Business Journal	230-8400
Today's Arizona Women Success Magazine (TAW)	945-5000
US West Home Office Consultant	630-0778

Business Setup Checklist

Business Entity (with advisor, select one)	Sole Proprietor Partnership, LLC Professional Corporation Corporation
	By-Laws Articles of Incorporation Corporation Commission
Federal	Employer Tax ID Number File SS-4 to get ID Number 941 - tax deposits (employee withholding) 940 - quarterly FUTA (Fed. Unemployment Tax)
State	State Withholding Number Joint Tax Application Dept. of Economic Security State Sales Tax City Sales Tax
Certifications And Permits	City License Number Home Occupation Permit Bonding Industry specific license WBE/MBE/DBE Certification
Insurance	Business Liability

	Homeowners Policy
Workers' Comp ID Number	
	State Fund, other
Bank Account	Checking account
	Market Interest/savings
	Line of Credit
	Corporate Credit card
Attorney	Business Agreements
	Contracts, Leases
	Employment Agreements
	Drug Testing
	Background Checking
Accountant	Accounting principles
	Method of reporting (cash, accrual)
	Estimated Income Taxes
	Quarterly Reports
	DES
	Federal
	State
	Workers Comp
	W-2's
	Business tax return
	Accounting Software

Business Plan

Plan to start and write your Plan

I've included the table of contents from my original business plan *(02/93)*. I really wasn't too sure of what I was doing, regarding the *correct* format and all, but it gave me something to work from. Maybe it will help you to get started. This is not meant in any way to define a business plan, but only to show you that it isn't as bad as you may think to write. Once you get started, you'll see what you need.

Here's a hint. Start with an overview. Pretend you are writing a marketing brochure about your very successful, five year old company. Define what you do and how well you do it. By describing how you "did it", you'll be writing your "how to do it" plan.

And remember, there are usually many service organizations around that can help you, **FREE**. Check with you local SCORE office (part of the SBA), your local Chamber of Commerce, and your state's Department of Commerce (in Phoenix, there is a separate Small Business Connection and a Women and Minority Office within the Department of Commerce). Many larger companies have special offices designed specifically to help small businesses.

From my original Business Plan (from 02/93).

Table of Contents

1.0 Overview
2.0 Approach
   2.1 Define Business Services
   2.2 Establish Infrastructure
   2.3 Establish Local Network
   2.4 Develop & Execute Marketing Plan
   2.5 Maintain Control of Expenses
3.0 Supporting Projects
4.0 Constraints
5.0 Summary
6.0 Appendices
   Appendix A
      Projected Budgets for 1993, 1994
   Appendix B
      Literature and Materials
   Appendix C
      PC Hardware and Software

Action Items

I wrote this action list to remind me of what I had to do - and put it in my business plan to make it seem more "official" for me. It helped me to establish my infrastructure; that is, what I really needed to do to get started. Write your own list and update it regularly. Some of these tasks may not apply to you.

(This is from my business plan 02/93)

Action Items
Completed and In Process

- Worker's Compensation certification is in process.
- Application for city permit for business has been approved (Glendale).
- Application for tradename has been approved (Secretary of State).
- Federal Tax ID number has been obtained.
- Advertising is currently in Arizona Republic, The Arrow (a local newspaper), and Deer Tracks (Deer Valley School District newspaper).

- Printer has been established in Glendale.

- Accountant has been established in Scottsdale.

- Bank accounts have been established with FIB in Glendale.

- Clients secured to date include a medical distributor and a telemarketing firm. In process of securing work with major bank and medical provider.

- Database of almost 200 prospective clients has been established and marketing literature has been distributed.

- Database of about 50 prospective, pre-screened staff consultants has been established.

- Agency relationships for recruiting have been established with several local and Southern California firms.

- Application has been received for membership in a women & minority association; planning to attend March event to evaluate.

- Application has been received for membership in the Phoenix Chamber of Commerce; have started to attend events to evaluate this group for membership.

- Discussions with three groups to provide free "Introduction to PCs" seminar; targeted seminars for early to mid-April. One seminar has been scheduled for April 8.

- Application for teaching has been submitted to Glendale Community Services, Parks and Recreation Department, for PC instruction (for summer sessions).

- Meetings are being arranged and attended with MIS management throughout the greater Phoenix area to begin the establishment of a strong client base.

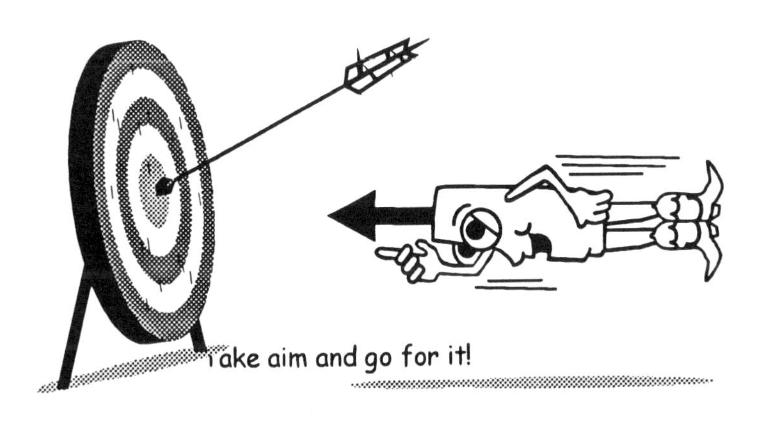

9 Who and What is RB Balch

Rochelle
Beth
Balch

In case you've been wondering, RB is me, Rochelle Beth. When I was *booted out*, and before I was really *committed* to starting my business, I spread the word that I was available. I told sales people at local computer stores that I was available to help people set up their computers and train them on various applications. Within a few days, I was getting calls! I hadn't even picked a name for my business, so, quickly, I printed up some business cards on my computer and called myself Balch & Associates. Then, when I filed for a tradename with the state, I found out that the name was already taken! I quickly changed to RB Balch & Associates and later incorporated and added the *Inc.*

I have been in the computer industry since 1968, starting as a keypunch operator and then becoming a programmer, an analyst, a project leader and information systems manager. I have been in the computer consulting business from 1979. I set up and managed consulting offices for two separate computer consulting firms for fifteen years, in Southern California, before starting my own company in Arizona.

I am a single mother with two daughters, Beth and Shayna (currently aged 12 and 13).

From the beginning, I have felt strongly about helping to create a stronger image for woman-owned (WBE) and minority (MBE) businesses, as well as for all home based business owners. I have testified for WBE's and MBE's at the city and state levels and have spoken at committee hearings and meetings for the rights for small business owners. The more success and recognition I receive personally and for my business, RB Balch, the more opportunities are available for me to try to encourage other men and women to (if appropriate), take the risk and start their own business.

Being downsized out of a job has certainly "upsized" me into being happy, successful and independent.

RB Balch & Associates, Inc. is a computer consulting firm. Initially, I went out and helped small businesses set up computers. Now, with over thirty employees, we provide contract programming (and some full time placement) services to large fortune 500 companies. Contract assignments with the larger firms are generally 6 to 12 months in length (and 40 to 50 hours per week) and are generally more profitable than business with smaller, micro businesses. This part of our business is by far the largest (about 90%).

However, we still provide as needed, on call services (usually 2 to 10 hours per week) to the smaller companies. We do this because there is a need; small, micro businesses, some home based, need good, reliable support and I believe that we should provide it. It is more difficult to manage, sometimes more difficult to collect the fees, and is not as profitable. But, it's how I got started and I want to continue to provide this service. Sometimes, as a business owner, you do things simply because you want to and because you should.

Since our employees, our "computer consultants", each work on different assignments, and many for different clients, developing a sense of a *team* and a *unified* company with many employees has been a challenge. The majority of my competitors assign the consultant to an account and the consultant may never meet other employees of the same firm.

So what do we do that is different? If the clients don't come together, then we have to bring our staff together. Quarterly, we invite all of our staff to lunch. In the beginning, our luncheons consisted of about a half dozen employees. Now, generally, 25 to 30 come. Sometimes, past employees even join us. It is so exciting to see this; this gives me a huge sense of accomplishment.

Oh yes, did I mention that we always have our luncheons on a payday and bring checks? This seems to encourage attendance. We also present anniversary gifts to our staff (our 1 year gift is a watch, 2 year gift is small radio, and soon, we'll need a 3 year gift). Of course, all gifts have our logo imprinted on them.

As the business grows, new situations occur. This is part of the fun of being a business owner. I like being creative. I like being able to, basically, do whatever I want to (I say basically because I do consult with Andy, Lori, and Karen, and sometimes—can you believe—we may not agree). I like facing challenges and solving problems. It's plain and simple—I just like being the *boss*.

As a result of a lot of marketing, visibility, and good service, we have created a successful business.

Our growth has been tremendous.

Sales, by year:

1st year, 1993	**$85,000**
2nd year, 1994	**$673,000**
3rd year, 1995	**$1,600,000**
4th year, 1996	**$2,200,000**
Est. for 1997	**$2,400,000**
Target for 1998	**$2,800,000**

Because of our marketing and success, we have received much recognition both statewide and nationally. And we're not bashful about telling people about our success. Over the next few pages, I've listed some of our community involvement and accomplishments (up to time of printing); perhaps this will give you some ideas. Go for it!

Accomplishments

AWARDS, RECOGNITION

Named, 1997 Honoree for Celebration of Success, Impact for Enterprising Women

Named, 1997 Arizona Ernst & Young LLP, Emerging Entrepreneur of the Year. *Nominated, 1995, 1996*

Named, 1996 National SOHO (Small Office Home Office) Winner, Entrepreneur Magazine and Office Depot, Presented in Ft. Lauderdale, FL

Named, 1996 Arizona Business Owner of the Year, NAWBO

Named, 1997, 1996 Top 100 Business Women, Today's Arizona Woman (TAW) Success Magazine & Deloitte Touche

Named, 1997 Top 25 Software Firms in the Valley, The Business Journal

Named, 1997 Top 10 Women in the High Technology Industry, TAW

Finalist, 1997 Athena Award (business), Arizona Chamber of Commerce

Finalist, 1996 Athena Award (individual), Phoenix Chamber of Commerce

Semi-finalist, 1997 Mastering Marketing Award, INC. Magazine

VOLUNTEER ACTIVITIES

Volunteer, Juvenile Justice Panel, Maricopa County, *from 04/97*

Volunteer, Arizona Grand Canyon State Games, volunteer headquarters coordinator, *1996, 1997*

Volunteer, Phoenix Hoop-It-Up, volunteer headquarters coordinator, *10/95, 10/96, 10/97*

Volunteer, AWEE (AZ Women Education & Employment), annual fundraising luncheon committee, *1996, 1997*

Volunteer, Junior Achievement, Instructor for elementary school bilingual classes, *school years 94/95, 95/96, 96/97*

Volunteer, Maricopa County Sheriffs Dept., Captain, Cyber Posse, *from 07/96*

Volunteer, Toyota Golf Challenge, trouble-shooter, *05/96*

Volunteer, Native American Festival, information booth, *03/96*

Volunteer, SCORE (Service Core Of Retired Executives, part of the SBA), part-time counselor, specializing in women-owned, home based and computer related issues for small businesses, *from 02/96*

Volunteer, Parent's Career Day, elementary and middle school, *1995, 1996*

Volunteer, Resource Expert, Information Technology Session, Arizona White House Conference on Small Business, *03/95*

Volunteer, NBA Jam Session, "Dream Team" staff supervisor, *02/95*

Volunteer, CASS (Central Arizona Shelter System), Men's and Family Shelters, "Preparing for a Job," *1994, 1995*

INVITED GUEST

Invited Speaker, ComputFest97, CompuFest96 and CompuFest95, for '95, '96 Sun City senior computer show; for '97 Glendale Community College, 5,000 attendees, seminars for 200 to 600. "Introduction to PCs" and "The Internet, What is it anyway?" *01/95, 02/96, 11/97*

Invited Panelist, Arizona Women '97 Conference, "The Power of One, Keys to starting a home based business", Governor's Division for Women, *10/97*

Invited Speaker, Impact for Enterprising Women, "Creating a successful image—Looking bigger than you are", *10/97*

Invited Speaker, Computer & Business Expo 1996 and 1997, Phoenix Civic Plaza, "Give your business the high tech edge", *10/96;* "Creating the image—looking bigger than you are", *10/97*

Invited Guest, Your Second Fifty Years, "Looking bigger than you are", Radio Station KMYL, 1190AM and 105.3FM, *09/13/97*

Invited Panelist, Small Business Forum, "Networking your way to the top", sponsored by Phoenix Chamber of Commerce, supported by many other city Chamber offices, *08/97*

Invited Speaker, Glendale Public Library, "Creating a successful image—Looking bigger than you are", *02/97, 08/97.* "Snap out of it and get hired!", "Give your business the hightech edge." *Scheduled 1998.*

Invited Speaker, Arizona Family Expo, Governor's Office for Women, "Employee issues", *05/95,* "Marketing strategies", *04/97*

Invited Speaker, ACM and IEEE, Phoenix Chapter, "Job market 1997", *03/97*

Invited Speaker, Arizona-Sonora Conference, Hermosillo, Sonora. Mexican government and the Arizona Dept.

of Commerce, presented in Spanish, "Home based & connecting to the world" *10/95;* "President, Mom, Volunteer: What more", *03/97*

Invited Guest, featured on FOX Channel 10 with Rick D'Amico, PrimeTime News, "Arizona's Most Successful Women", 4 ½ minute segment, *11/13/96;* "Where the Jobs Are" (Channel 10 and Arizona Dept. of Economic Security (AZ DES), *01/11/97*

Invited Speaker, Entrepreneurial Mothers Association, "C-E- O and M-O-M, Same Time, Same Place", East Valley Chapter, *11/96*

Invited Panelist, Maricopa County HR, "Re-entering the work force", *06/96*

Invited Speaker, UMOM (United Methodist Outreach Ministry), Role Modeling Program, *03/96*

Invited Speaker, Western Entrepreneurs Conference, "Introduction to the Information Super Highway", *1995*

Invited Speaker, Paradise Valley College Job Club, "Interviewing", "Resume Writing", "Networking for a job", *1995, 1996*

Invited Guest, "Getting Acquainted with Glendale", Glendale Cable TV, representing Glendale Parks and Recreation Department, PC class, 0*4/94*

FEATURED, WRITER

Business 97 (national), featured, "Customer Focus", Wells Fargo small business magazine, *October 1997*

The Arizona Republic, featured, front page business section, "Networking to success, Forum offers entrepreneurs tips that work", *08/29/97*

The Business Journal, featured, "Balch's home based business emerges on top", *06/26/97*

Business 97 (national), included, Internet issue, Wells Fargo small business magazine, *June/July 1997*

Today's Arizona Woman Success Magazine, guest writer, Heart & Spirit in Business, "Scattered employees join together", *May 1997*

PriceCostco Business Connection (national), featured, "To Give is to Receive", *May 1997*

Independent Business (national), included, Web issue, NFIB magazine, *January/February 1997*

Entrepreneur Magazine (national), featured, Winners - Women of the Year, "Power Surge", *January 1997*

The Arizona Republic, featured, front page business section, "For entrepreneur, it's home sweet home", *12/18/96*

Jewish News, guest writer, Business & Finance special, "Save time, money with high tech", *06/28/96*

Jewish News, guest writer, Business & Finance special, "Home based businesses can be fun, profitable", PC related articles, *06/30/95*

Arrowhead Independent, featured, front page, "Ranch Resident - No place like home", *06/05/96*

Arizona Business Gazette, included, On-line Office magazine, "Thousands of firms find home on Internet", *December 1995*

Primera Plana, Mexican newspaper, featured, "Restan seriedad en Mexico a las microempresarias" translated "Mexico needs to consider women business owners more seriously", *10/27/95*

The Arrow, featured, Who's News?, "Resident hits record $1 million in sales", *09/13/95*

The Business Gazette, featured, front page small business section, "Giving edge to women, minorities", *12/15/94*

OTHER

Member, Phoenix Chamber of Commerce, *from 1993*

Member, Glendale Chamber of Commerce, *from 1996*

Member, Arizona Chamber of Commerce, *from 1996*

Member, Board Member ('95), NAWBO (National Association of Women Business Owners), *from 1993*

Named to GSPED (Governor's Strategic Partnership for Economic Development), Minority & Small Business Commission, Executive Council, *94/95*

Instructor, "How to Buy a Computer", "Introduction to PC's", "Professional Resume Writing", "Interviewing Techniques", "Introduction to Windows", "Starting a Home Based Business", "The Information Superhighway - What is it anyway", Glendale Parks & Recreation Department, *from 06/93*

Certified WBE (Woman-Owned Business Enterprise), by City of Phoenix, Maricopa County, Arizona Dept. of Transportation, *from 1993*

Sponsor, Girls and Boys Softball League, City of Glendale, Parks and Recreation Dept, *summer 1997*

Sponsor, 1996, 1997 (Bronze), 1998 (Silver) Arizona Grand Canyon State Games, Summer and Winter Games, Family Rodeo (main sponsor)

Awards
Speaker
Recognition
Volunteer
HEY!!

10 Start Now, Take Notes

Start thinking about yourself and what you want to do. If you get any ideas while reading, write it down! This could be an easy way to start your business plan.

Notes

Notes

MY
BUSINESS
INC.

Call Me: (602) 561-9366

Fax Me: (602) 561-0012

See Me: www.rbbalch.com

E Me$_{tm}$: rb@rbbalch.com

RB Balch & Associates, Inc.
PO BOX 10007
Glendale, AZ 85318-0007

Order a copy for a friend.

C-E-O & M-O-M

Same Time, Same Place

$9.95, plus $2.95 for shipping and handling (total $12.90). A portion of all book sales will be donated to a local victim's shelter for women. Thank you.

Please make check payable to RB Balch & Associates, Inc. and send check or money order to:

C-E-O & M-O-M
C/O RB Balch
PO Box 10007
Glendale, AZ 85318-0007

Copy this form or be sure to include your name and address for shipping.

Name ________________________________

Address ______________________________

City ___________ State _____ Zip ______

Phone (optional) (_____) ________________

Howdy. Have fun! See ya. Adios. Later dude.